On Thursday evening, December 1, 1955, Rosa Parks left work and started home. She was tired. "Today, I'll ride the bus," she thought.

She got on and sat in the first seat for blacks, right behind the white section. After a few stops the seats were filled. A white man got on. He looked for an empty seat. Then he looked at the driver. The driver came over to Mrs. Parks.

"You have to get up," he said.

All of a sudden Mrs. Parks knew she was not going to give up her seat. This time she was not going to move.

Rosa Parks

Rosa Parks

by Eloise Greenfield
illustrated by Gil Ashby

HarperTrophy®

*A Division of HarperCollins**Publishers***

Acknowledgments

A very special thanks to Mrs. Johnnie R. Carr of Montgomery, Alabama, for her generosity in sharing with me her childhood memories of Mrs. Parks.

Material on pages 1, 7, 8, 15, and 18 from *Black Profiles* by George R. Metcalf, copyright 1970 by George R. Metcalf, has been used by permission of the McGraw-Hill Book Company.

Material on pages 9 and 10 from the Truman R. Temple interview with Rosa Parks in *The Washington Star*, copyright 1965, The Washington Star, has been reprinted by permission.

Harper Trophy® is a registered trademark
of HarperCollins Publishers Inc.

Newly illustrated edition.
LC Number 95-35497
Trophy ISBN 0-06-442025-6
First HarperTrophy edition, 1995.

15 16 OPM 30 29

For my grandson,
Michael

Rosa Parks

Chapter One

Rosa was not afraid, although the white boy was near his mother. When he pushed her, Rosa pushed him back.

"Why did you put your hands on my child?" the mother asked.

"Because he pushed me," Rosa said.

"Don't you know that I could have you put in jail?" the mother asked.

Rosa answered, "I don't want to be pushed by your son or anyone else."

And she walked on.

That was in Montgomery, the capital of Alabama, where Rosa lived. She was a child then, and not many people knew her. But after she grew up, everyone in Montgomery and people all over the United States and the world would know about Rosa Parks.

Chapter Two

Rosa was born in Tuskegee, Alabama, not far from Montgomery, on February 4, 1913. Her name was Rosa McCauley then. Her parents were James and Leona McCauley. Mr. McCauley was a carpenter. Mrs. McCauley had once been a teacher.

When Rosa was still very small, her family moved to a little farm at the edge of Montgomery. There, she lived with her mother and her grandparents and her younger brother, Sylvester. Her father had moved to another city.

Rosa attended the Montgomery Industrial School for Girls. She was a quiet little girl who liked to read. One of her favorite classes was sewing, where she made aprons, handkerchiefs, and easy-to-sew dresses for herself.

In Montgomery, Alabama, and all over the South, there were groups of white men called the Ku Klux Klan. Sometimes they were called the KKK. These men were cowards. They wore white hoods over their heads to hide their faces and white sheets

around their bodies. They wanted black people to be slaves. So they would set fire to the homes and schools of black people. They would also drag people from their homes and kill them.

Sometimes at night, Rosa would not go to bed. She knew that at any minute the KKK might break into her home and beat up or kill the whole family. So she sat up, listening and waiting with her grandfather, who kept his shotgun nearby. The KKK never came, but Rosa stayed awake many nights.

Black people had other problems in Alabama. There were special rules that they had to live by. Rosa did not like these rules at all. She did not like having to drink out of special water fountains in public places. But

some were for white people only. She did not like the old, crowded schools that most black children went to while the white children went to new schools.

And when Rosa found out that she could not eat or drink at the food counters in the downtown stores, she did not like that, either.

One day she and her cousin, Annie Mae Williamson, were shopping. They were thirsty and went into a five-and-ten-cent store. Annie Mae asked for a soda.

The white saleswoman said, "I'll sell you an ice-cream cone."

The saleswoman meant that she could eat the cone outside and would not have to

sit at the counter. But Annie Mae did not understand. She asked for a soda three times. Then the saleswoman leaned over and whispered, "We don't sell sodas to colored people."

"Well, why didn't you tell me that in the first place?" Annie Mae asked angrily as she and Rosa left.

Chapter Three

With her mother's help, Rosa was able to grow up proud of herself and other black people, even while living with these rules. Her mother taught her not to judge people by the amount of money they had or the kinds of houses they lived in or the clothes they wore.

People should be judged by the respect they have for themselves and others, Mrs. McCauley said. Rosa grew up believing this. It helped her to do the hard things that she had to do later in life.

After she graduated from junior high school, Rosa took some high school courses at Alabama State College. It was a different kind of college. It was for students of all ages, from nursery school through college.

Later Rosa worked at several jobs. She had grown up to be a lovely young woman. She had a quiet, gentle way of talking and moving, and sparkling, brown eyes. A few weeks before her twentieth birthday, she married Raymond Parks, a barber. Rosa McCauley became Mrs. Rosa Parks.

Many years had passed since Mrs. Parks was a child, but Montgomery still had special rules for black people. And Mrs. Parks still did not like them. In spite of her gentle ways, she still believed in defending herself. Now she decided that she would defend herself and her people, too.

She joined the NAACP, a group of people

who work to get better houses and jobs for black people. They also send lawyers into court to help black people who have been treated unfairly.

Some NAACP members are teen-agers. Many times, after working all day, Mrs. Parks would meet with the teen-agers of the Montgomery NAACP. She would help them learn about the problems of their city. Sometimes she would work as secretary to Edgar Daniel Nixon. Mr. Nixon was president of the Montgomery NAACP.

Mrs. Parks also joined the Montgomery Voters League. The members of the league wanted all black people to vote. Mrs. Parks visited the homes of black people teaching them how to pass the voting test. They had to pass the test without one mistake to have their names placed on the voting lists.

Many white people did not want black people to vote. They said that blacks who tried to vote would lose their jobs or have to move from their homes. But the black people were brave. They knew that they had as much right to vote as the whites.

As much as she could, Mrs. Parks refused to go along with the unfair rules the city had made. When she was downtown, she walked up and down the stairs rather than ride elevators marked "Colored." On hot days when her throat was dry, she walked past the water fountains marked "Colored."

Often she walked the mile from home to work and the mile back again from work to home rather than ride the bus. For the buses were worst of all.

A black person who wanted to ride the bus had to get on at the front door and pay his fare. Then he had to get off, go to the back door, and get on again. Sometimes the driver would drive away before the person had time to get back on.

If he could get on the bus, the person was allowed to sit only in certain seats. The seats in the front half were for whites. The seats in the back were for blacks.

Whenever a white person got on the bus and found no empty seat, the driver would go to the black people sitting nearest the front.

"Hey, you," he would say, "get up and let this white man sit down."

And the people would have to get up. The law said that the driver was the king of the bus.

Mrs. Parks felt as if something inside her died a little each time she had to ride the bus. She felt especially sad because of the little children.

A child would run on the bus ahead of his mother and sit down. If he sat in the wrong part of the bus, his mother would pull him up and move quickly to the back before the driver yelled at them. The child would ask, "Why can't we sit there, Mama?" But the mother would have no answer.

Chapter Four

Rosa Parks had often been mistreated by bus drivers. Once, she decided not to get on at the back door. She paid her fare and started down the aisle. The driver ran after her, snatched hold of her, and pulled her to the door. Then he pushed her out and drove away.

One spring day a fifteen-year-old girl refused to stand up and give her seat to a white man. The bus driver called the police, and three policemen handcuffed the teenager and carried her out. She was kicking and screaming.

When the black people of Montgomery heard about this, they became very angry.

"We've got to do something," they said. But no one could decide just what to do.

Not long afterward, another driver got so angry with a young black man that he beat him in the face with a piece of metal. The man had to go to the hospital. The driver was arrested.

Rosa Parks went to court to watch the driver's trial. He was found guilty and had to pay a twenty-five dollar fine, but he did not lose his job.

Again the black citizens were angry. Still, no one knew what to do.

Chapter Five

By now, Mrs. Parks had a job sewing in a department store. When people bought dresses or suits that did not fit, Mrs. Parks made them a little longer or shorter or tighter or looser.

On Thursday evening, December 1, 1955, Mrs. Parks left work and started home. She was tired. Her shoulders ached from bending over the sewing machine all day. "Today, I'll ride the bus," she thought.

She got on and sat in the first seat for blacks, right behind the white section. After a few stops the seats were filled. A white man got on. He looked for an empty seat.

Then he looked at the driver. The driver came over to Mrs. Parks.

"You have to get up," he said.

All of a sudden Mrs. Parks knew she was not going to give up her seat. It was not fair. She had paid her money just as the man had. This time she was not going to move.

"No," she said softly.

"You'd better get up, or I'll call the police," the driver said.

It was very quiet on the bus now. Everyone stopped talking and watched. Still, Mrs. Parks did not move.

"Are you going to get up?"

"No," she repeated.

The driver left the bus and returned with two policemen.

"You're under arrest," they told her.

Mrs. Parks walked off the bus. The

policemen put her in their car and drove to the police station. One policeman stuck a camera in her face and took her picture. Another took her fingerprints. Then she was locked in a cell.

Mrs. Parks felt very bad, sitting in that little room with iron bars. But she did not cry. She was a religious woman, and she thought of her faith in God. She said a silent prayer. Then she waited.

Someone who had seen Mrs. Parks arrested called Edgar Daniel Nixon of the NAACP. Mr. Nixon went right away to the police station and posted a hundred dollar bond for Mrs. Parks. This meant that she could leave, but that she promised to go to court on Monday for her trial.

Mrs. Parks left the police station. She had been locked up for two and a half hours. Mr.

Nixon drove her home. At her apartment Mrs. Parks, her husband, Mr. Nixon, and Fred Gray, a lawyer, talked about what had happened. They thought they saw a way to solve the problem of the buses.

Mr. Gray would go into court with Mrs. Parks. He would prove that the bus company was not obeying the United States Constitution. The Constitution is an important paper that was written by the men who started the United States. It says that all the citizens of the United States must be treated fairly.

The next morning Mrs. Parks went to her job as usual. Her employer was surprised to see her. He had read about her arrest in the newspaper, and he thought she would be too upset to come in. Some of the white workers gave Mrs. Parks mean looks and would not speak to her. But she went on with her work.

That night Mrs. Parks met with a group of ministers and other black leaders of the city. Dr. Martin Luther King was one of the ministers. The black men and women of Montgomery were angry again. But this time they knew what to do.

"If the bus company won't treat us courteously," one leader said, "we won't spend our money to ride the buses. We'll walk!"

After the meeting some of the people printed little sheets of paper. These sheets of paper, called leaflets, said, "DON'T RIDE THE BUS TO WORK, TO TOWN, TO SCHOOL, OR ANYWHERE, MONDAY, DECEMBER 5." They also invited people to a church meeting on Monday night. The leaflets were left everywhere—in mail boxes, on porches, in drugstores.

Chapter Six

On Sunday morning black ministers all over the city preached about Rosa Parks in their churches. Dr. King preached from his pulpit at the Dexter Avenue Baptist Church.

The preachers said, "Brothers and sisters, if you don't like what happened to Rosa Parks and what has been happening to us all these years, do something about it. Walk!"

And the people said, "Amen. We'll walk."

On Monday morning, no one was riding the buses. There were many people on the street, but everyone was walking. They were cheering because the buses were empty.

Mrs. Parks got up early that morning. She went to court with her lawyer for her trial. The judge found her guilty. But she and her lawyer did not agree with him. Her lawyer said, "We'll get a higher court to decide. If we have to, we'll take the case to the highest court in the United States."

That night thousands of people went to the church meeting. There were so many people that most of them had to stand outside and listen through a loudspeaker.

First there was prayer. Then Rosa Parks was introduced. She stood up slowly. The audience rose to its feet and clapped and cheered. After Mrs. Parks sat down, several ministers gave their speeches. Finally Dr. Martin Luther King started to speak.

"We are tired," he said.

"Yes, Lord," the crowd answered.

"We are tired of being kicked around," he said.

"Yes, Lord," they answered.

"We're not going to be kicked around anymore," Dr. King said. "We walked one day. Now we are going to have a real protest. We are going to keep walking until the bus company gives us fair treatment."

After Dr. King finished speaking, the Montgomery Improvement Association was formed to plan the protest. Dr. King was made president.

Then there was hymn singing and hand clapping. The people went home feeling good. All that walking was not going to be easy, but they knew they could do it.

Chapter Seven

The Montgomery Improvement Association and the churches bought as many cars and station wagons as they could afford. There were telephone numbers that people could call when they needed a ride. Women who worked at home answered the phones. Mrs. Parks was one of them. Her employer had told her that she was no longer needed. When someone called for a ride, Mrs. Parks would tell the drivers where to go. But there were not nearly enough cars.

Old people and young people walked. The children walked a long way to school. The men and women walked to work, to church, everywhere. In the morning it was like a parade. People were going to work,

some riding on the backs of mules, some riding in wagons pulled by horses, but most of them walking. Sometimes they sang.

In the evening the parade went the other way, people going home. The newspapers called Montgomery "the walking city."

It was hard. Many people had to leave home long before daylight to get to work on time. They got home late at night. Their feet hurt. But they would not give up. The bus company kept saying it would not change. And black people kept on walking.

The enemies of the black people tried to frighten them. They threw bottles at the walkers. Some homes were bombed.

One day Mrs. Parks's phone rang. She picked it up.

"Hello," she said.

"You're the cause of all this trouble," a

voice said. "You should be killed."

Mrs. Parks hung up. The calls kept coming, day after day. Mrs. Parks was afraid, but she knew she could not stop.

After two months, more than a hundred leaders of the protest were arrested. Mrs. Parks was among them. A court had said that the protest was against the law. The leaders posted bond and went right back to their work.

Reporters came to Montgomery from all over the United States and from other countries. They wrote stories in their newspapers about the arrests.

Mrs. Parks began to travel to other cities, making speeches. She told about the hardships of the people. Many of the people she spoke to helped. They gave her money to pay for bonds and to buy gas for the cars.

The black citizens of Montgomery walked all winter, all spring, all summer and fall in all kinds of weather. The bus company lost thousands of dollars.

In November, the Supreme Court, the highest court in the United States, said that the bus company had to change. It had not been obeying the Constitution.

That night the Ku Klux Klan paraded past the homes of the black people. The people stood in their doorways and watched. They were no longer afraid. They had won.

Several weeks later, the bus company obeyed the Supreme Court and changed its rules. A year had passed since Rosa Parks refused to give up her seat. Now black people could sit in any seat. They would not have to get up for anyone.

Chapter Eight

Black people in other places read about Montgomery. More and more of them began to work for fair treatment in their own cities.

They said, "If Rosa Parks had the courage to do this, we can do it too." They called her "the Mother of the Civil Rights Movement."

One day a group of reporters went to Mrs. Parks's home. They took her to ride on the bus. She entered through the front door. For the first time she sat anywhere she chose. And she would stay there until the end of her ride.

No one could ever ask her to get up again.

A Note from the Author

December 1, 1995, marks the fortieth anniversary of the famous refusal of Rosa Parks to give in to injustice. Her refusal, the year-long protest that followed it, and the part of the Civil Rights Movement that grew from it have an important place in the long history of the African-American struggle for freedom and justice.

The struggle began when the first Africans were kidnapped from their homelands, imprisoned on ships, and taken to live and work, still as prisoners, in lands far away from the people they loved. They ran away, they fought, they helped each other to escape. They studied in secret and learned to read, knowing they would be whipped or worse if they were caught. Those who were free made speeches, started newspapers, and wrote letters to Congress.

Even after the period called Slavery was over, the struggle did not stop. African Americans met with Congress, became members of Congress, started their own schools, and marched for their rights. They wanted an end to the killings, they wanted jobs and the right to rent or buy homes wherever they chose. I remember, in the 1940s, seeing lines of people, in Washington, D.C., where I lived, walking up and down with picket signs in front of theaters and restaurants to which they were not allowed to go.

The work of Rosa Parks was a part of all

of this. Others such as Sojourner Truth, Frederick Douglass, Harriet Tubman, and Martin Luther King, Jr., in their times, were a part of all of this. When we think of them, we think of their dedication and courage. When we call their names, when we honor them, we honor also the thousands and thousands of other courageous people whose names we will never know.

Eloise Greenfield
February 1995

TROPHY CHAPTER BOOKS YOU WILL ENJOY:

Danger Guys
by Tony Abbott

Danger Guys Blast Off
by Tony Abbott

**Danger Guys:
Hollywood Halloween**
by Tony Abbott

Danger Guys Hit the Beach
by Tony Abbott

Danger Guys On Ice
by Tony Abbott

Pirate's Promise
by Clyde Robert Bulla

The Secret Valley
by Clyde Robert Bulla

Shoeshine Girl
by Clyde Robert Bulla

Seven Treasure Hunts
by Betsy Byars

**One Day in the
Tropical Rain Forest**
by Jean Craighead George

One Day in the Woods
by Jean Craighead George

In a Messy, Messy Room
by Judith Gorog

Rosa Parks
by Eloise Greenfield

**Jason and the Aliens Down
the Street**
by Gery Greer and Bob Ruddick

**Jason and the Escape from
Bat Planet**
by Gery Greer and Bob Ruddick

Riches
by Esther Hautzig

Dracula Is a Pain in the Neck
by Elizabeth Levy

**Frankenstein Moved in on the
Fourth Floor**
by Elizabeth Levy

**Gorgonzola Zombies
in the Park**
by Elizabeth Levy

Rude Rowdy Rumors
by Elizabeth Levy

School Spirit Sabotage
by Elizabeth Levy

The Adam Joshua Capers
by Janice Lee Smith:

**#1 The Monster in the Third
Dresser Drawer**

#2 The Kid Next Door

#3 Superkid!

#4 The Show-and-Tell War

#5 The Halloween Monster

#6 George Takes a Bow-Wow!

#7 Turkey Trouble

#8 The Christmas Ghost

Go Fish
by Mary Stolz

Stepbrother Sabotage
by Sally Wittman

Pudmuddles
by Carol Beach York